Smart Mouth

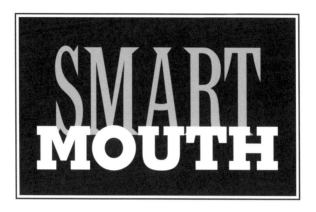

Poetry & Prose by
WritersCorps Youth

INTRODUCTION BY
JUSTIN CHIN

ART BY
GABRIELLE GAMBOA
ANSON JEW
DEREK KIRK
NINA PALEY
SPAIN RODRIGUEZ

*Writers*Corps
BOOKS

An earlier version of Sarah A.'s poem, "Keeping It Real,"
first appeared in *The Beat Within*, a weekly newsletter
of writing and artwork by incarcerated youth in
Northern California, published by Pacific News Service.

ISBN: 1-888048-05-0

WritersCorps Editorial Team:
Valerie Chow Bush, Managing Editor
Janet Heller, WritersCorps Project Manager
Michelle Matz, WritersCorps Teacher
Robert Allen, WritersCorps Advisory Board Member

Bill Prochnow, Art Director/Designer

1999-2000 WritersCorps Teachers: Cathy Arellano,
Ananda Esteva, Russell (Gonzaga), Michelle Matz,
Kimberley Nelson, Alison Seevak

The San Francisco WritersCorps, a project of the San
Francisco Arts Commission, places writers in community
settings to teach creative writing to youth. The program is part
of a national alliance, with sites in the Bronx and Washington,
D.C., whose shared vision is to transform and strengthen
individuals and communities through the written word.

WritersCorps gratefully acknowledges the support of the
Mayor's Department of Children, Youth and Their Families;
The Department of Juvenile Probation; The Walter and
Elise Haas Fund; The National Endowment for the Arts;
The Richard and Rhoda Goldman Fund; Borders Books
and Music; The Gap, Inc.; and individuals.
For more information, please call 415-252-4655.

www.writerscorps-sf.org

For every

smart mouth

who gets

it down

on paper

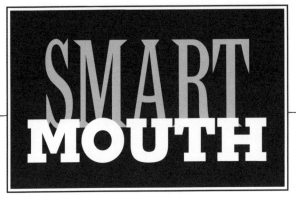

contents

"Nose Like a Tuna"
by Anson Jew
Page 2

CHAPTER TWO: NEVER SAFE

"Frostbite"
by Nina Paley
Page 30

CHAPTER THREE: I AM EVERYTHING TO ME

"The Grey Area"
by Gabrielle Gamboa
Page 80

CHAPTER FOUR: SEEING CLEARLY

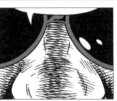

"Hurdles"
by Derek Kirk
Page 108

CHAPTER FIVE: THIS MUST NOT GET LOST
Teachers' Writings

"Wandering Home
to the Mission"
by Spain Rodriguez
Page 138

Foreword

SAN FRANCISCO WRITERSCORPS is pleased to bring you its sixth annual anthology, *Smart Mouth*, a marvelous collection of writing by young people who participated in our 1999–2000 program. WritersCorps, a part of the San Francisco Arts Commission since 1994, places writers in communities where primarily low-income, incarcerated, immigrant, homeless, or educationally disadvantaged youth live, work, or attend school. Teaching creative writing to nearly a thousand young people each year, WritersCorps provides long-term and in-depth workshops, positive role models, and lasting relationships.

The WritersCorps anthologies present a wide variety of literary work that reflects the contemporary concerns and lives of our young writers. This year we also invited local cartoonists to add their voices to the mix by creating drawings about childhood and adolescence from their unique points of view. The drawings function as segues through the many chapters of growing up—how we all deal with changing bodies, minds, attitudes, and the world around us.

WritersCorps believes strongly that children and youth must cultivate a "smart mouth" if they are to survive, flourish, and positively influence the world. When young people are given thoughtful instruction and the tools to write, the results are extraordinary. They shine with imaginative brilliance, feel the power of facing risk, and take real satisfaction in being heard and understood. In *Smart Mouth*, we take pleasure in sharing their experiences and their words with you.

Janet Heller, Project Manager

Introduction

AS PUNISHMENT FOR TALKING BACK, my mother and my guardians had a variety of punishments: canings on the tongue (really); rubbing cut chili peppers on the offending mouth; or just a good plain old spanking. When I grew older, a solid smack across the face sufficed.

Being smart-mouthed was not something a good filial Chinese boy did. The simple act of speaking was a minefield of decorum and etiquette. There were things I was not supposed to talk about (sex, family business failures, dissenting political opinions, the foibles of any relative) and words I wasn't supposed to say. One false move and Great Shame would be brought upon the family and me.

I was no angel. In my youth, I believed that I was old enough to make my own decisions. I could not understand why the adults in my life—parents and teachers—would not let me have my freedom. I rebelled like crazy: I stayed out all night with my friends, did badly in school, and acted out in so many self-destructive ways.

"You just don't understand," I yelled more than once; and my mom yelled back, "Well, make me understand!" But, smart mouth or not, I never could.

In negotiating the rocky terrain of my adolescence, all I could do was write in my notebook. I wrote of my joys, my hurt, my doomed relationships, my failing grades, my sense of despair, and worries about my future. I wrote of my growing passion for literature. In my writing, I could vent and spew and be as free in my speech and thoughts as I dared imagine. Writing these things gave them the weight and gravity that no one else in the world seemed to want to assign to them. Writing made the harshest things in my life bearable. And it continues to do so to this very day.

Reading the work of the young writers of *Smart Mouth* renews my conviction in the importance of writing. I am reminded of the value of telling even the simplest stories, describing the simplest things in one's life—the tingle of a favorite food, the familiar panorama of home life, the omnipresent yet ever-changing chalkboard in the classroom.

This modestly slim book is bursting with smartness, in mouth and in heart. In their writings, these young people explore how they fit in, and how the world should fit around them. They tackle the perplexing issues of identity, love, and loss. They take on the stuff of their lives: becoming a woman, the first rush of fatherhood, exile and displacement, violence and gangs, the meaning of being a good person.

I cannot imagine what it's like to be a young person in America these days. There is so much chaos and strife, so much to make sense of and to articulate. Yet the writers in *Smart Mouth* speak defiantly, loudly, and smartly in the face of the dominant babble. They are fearless enough to articulate this simple but indomitable fact: This is my life and it matters because I matter.

Justin Chin

Justin Chin is the author of *Mongrel: Essays, Diatribes & Pranks* and *Bite Hard*. He was a WritersCorps teacher in 1994, the program's inaugural year.

ONE

The
House
in Me

©2000 ANSON JEW

The House in Me

There is a house in me.
I go in the house when I am sad.
I go in the house when I am lonely.
I go in when I am afraid.
I go in when I am mad.
I talk to my imaginary friends.
They tell me how to do this and that.
The house is my feelings
and I will never let anyone
take it away from me.
I own it and it will last forever.

Lily Nguyen, 10
1028 Howard Street Apartments, Mercy Services

Left Out

Left Out lives in a dark house by himself.
His favorite color is black because it's how he's always feeling.
He eats leftovers, food from the garbage,
       and spinach that no one wants to eat.
Left Out doesn't have any friends.
Actually, he has one friend, Sadness.
Left Out likes to watch TV.
He likes to jump rope by himself and count his jumps.
He likes to count the bricks of his house.
When it's dark, Left Out cuddles in his little tiny blanket with his teddy.
When he sleeps, he dreams that he gets along with the other kids.

Angel Allen, 10, Cierra Crowell, 7, Saman Minapara, 7,
Ethel Lovely Lopez, 11, Elizabeth Marroquin, 10, Grace Sizelove, 9
Columbia Park Apartments, Mercy Services

A Beautiful Painting

When I close my eyes,
I see the color black,
my hair.
I see people.
When I open my eyes,
I see my bedroom
in my real house.
I got dolls on my bed.

When I dream,
I see people talking
and lots of things
like backpacks, clothes,
shoes, games, and knockers.

When I paint,
I see the color yellow
and the shape of squares.
I take a picture of my cousins,
Carolyn, Nikki, Jaleshia, and Lakeiya,
and my friends, Keri and Iris.
I paint flowers and butterflies.

I see through the future:
my family
and what I am going to be
like an artist, teacher,
and veterinarian.
It will look like
a beautiful painting.

Nichelle Fullbright, 10
Girls After School Academy

The Bus with Big Wheels

In my house
I smell Mexican food,
scrambled eggs,
orange-smelling perfume,
a dirty apartment,
onions frying.

I see my little sister,
the hot oven,
Winnie the Pooh,
the color television,
and Pokémon toys.

I feel the warm heater,
the bed,
my toys,
the fun books,
and yellow pointy pencils.

I hear yelling,
rock music,
orange cars,
the garbage man,
and the bus with big wheels.

I taste cheesy pizza,
fish,
bread,
sweet candy,
and yellow and white eggs.

Jocelyn Escobedo, 9
Career Resources Development Center

Monkey

I have a monkey
inside of me
because I like bananas
and I'm wild.

When somebody
calls me names about my hair
my monkey tells me
to ignore it.

Angel Allen, 10
Columbia Park Apartments, Mercy Services

My Friend

I see you there.
I see you there in my kindergarten class.
I spill the juice and it is spreading all over.
I know the teacher is coming back
and then I see you there,
helping me.

I see you at recess.
Nobody that I can play with
and I feel so cold.
But you ask me to play
and I feel warm again.

Lily Nguyen, 10
1028 Howard Street Apartments, Mercy Services

Lose

When I lost my big colorful bird
I felt very sad.
Then I told my mom that I lost my bird and she told me
to remember the fun we had together,
and I felt happy again.

At night when I am sleeping,
I dream of my bird.
In the morning my bird comes back to me.

Michelle Ha, 11
Career Resources Development Center

I Remember

I remember when my dad lived with me.
I remember when I threw a chicken bone at my sister's friend's head.
I remember when my mom took her cat for a walk and then came home.
I remember when I was born.
I remember when I thought Santa Claus was a ghost.

Cierra Crowell, 7
Columbia Park Apartments, Mercy Services

How Would You Save Her?

If she was in the water,
I would get her out of the water.

If she was choking,
I would pat her back.

If she was sad,
I would play games with her,
and go out to eat,
or something.

If she was doing bad things,
I would tell her to stop,
and tell her the right things to do.

If she thought she was ugly,
I would tell her,
"You are very pretty and intelliegnt."

If I were her,
I would help myself.

Marlesha Wilson, 10
Girls After School Academy

Passion for Pizza

On Wednesdays,
when my grandma
goes to bingo,
my mom makes
me and my cousins
some French bread pizza.
I get to help her.
She puts on the tomato sauce
and I put on my own toppings.
I put on some
cheese,
pepperoni,
olives,
and pineapple.
I like to eat pizza
at dinner
and for lunch.

Soyhala Andrews, 7
Girls After School Academy

Poetry

Poetry is like my mom's
vase that just fell and
broke. I have to put
the pieces back together,
but I don't know where
they belong.

Jacqueline Beck, 10
1028 Howard Street Apartments, Mercy Services

Black As the Dark

I am as black as the dark.
I am fried chicken.
I am a drum roll.
I am the smell of a burger.
I am a tiger roaring.
When I am mad,
I am a swamp with an alligator.

Luis Fernando Cortez, 7
1101 Howard Street Apartments, Mercy Services

Tomato

I hate tomatoes.
They're too healthy
for me.
They're not mouthwatering
like chocolate.
When I cut a tomato
all the juice
comes out
and makes the tomato
look like it spilled.
I don't like tomatoes.

Issielle Johnson, 9
Career Resources Development Center

I Lost

I lost my Pokémon cards because my little brother played with them.
I lost my library card because my mom doesn't know where she put it.
I lost my pencil at school and I do not know where it is.
I lost my best friend at school because she has a new friend.
I lost my book and I liked that book.

Lina Ton, 9
Career Resources Development Center

My Heart

My heart is like a strawberry,
a lion roaring,
like a sunflower dancing in the grass.
My heart is beeping like the sun,
moving like the water.
My heart is wiggling like a fish.

Tommy Nguyen, 8
1101 Howard Street Apartments, Mercy Services

Ode to Peacock Ore

Peacock Ore,
you are like a beautiful peacock.
When it's night, you shine like a star.
Peacock Ore, you are like a rainbow in the sky.
You are like my mom's favorite earrings.
Sometimes when you get mad, I talk to you.
You look like a little mountain.
You look like a triangle.
When it's morning,
you, the mountain, stand up and want to yawn.
I imagine that you are my favorite friend,
Peacock Ore.

Mina Vuong, 10
1028 Howard Street Apartments, Mercy Services

Generations of Love

My grandma taught me to cook when I was seven years old
    and helping her.
Her mama taught her and her mama's mama taught her.
I want one of my recipes in a cookbook.
I like to cook lemon shrimp because it tastes crunchy, juicy,
    spicy, and tender.
Here is the recipe for Lemon Shrimp:

Buy 5 pounds of shrimp.
Put the shrimp in the flour.
Put them in the skillet.
Fry them for 20 minutes.
If you want them to be crunchy
then put 1/2 cup of honey.
Add some pepper,
lemon spice,
1 slice of lemon,
a few sprinkles of sugar,
and salt.
Then mix well.
And you have your sauce.

Lorna Jackson, 11
Girls After School Academy

Song

A poem sounds like song.
A poem sounds like wind blowing.
A poem sounds like winter coming.
A poem sounds like poem trees shaking.

Saman Minapara, 7
Columbia Park Apartments, Mercy Services

My Brother

My brother's name is Avery.
When he sleeps, he sounds like a foghorn.
His head is shaped like a big orange.
His nose is as big as a small peach.
My brother's love is stronger than a blizzard.
I love my brother and my brother loves me
and that can never change.

Grace Sizelove, 9
Columbia Park Apartments, Mercy Services

Haiku

Sun and moon,
bright and dark,
again and again every day.

Joseph Beck, 11
1028 Howard Street Apartments, Mercy Services

My Mom

Her arms are two doors I go in
so she can give me a hug.
She is a cherry on the cherry
tree I planted.
Her lips are two apples that I eat.
Her laugh is like the wind
blowing in front of me.

Samantha Cortez, 9
1101 Howard Street Apartments, Mercy Services

Shiny Coin

Poetry is like a coin
that is shiny
that you hold
and it might
turn into a dollar
when you add
four 25 cents together
and then your friend
will want you
to spend it
to buy a toy.

Phillip Nguyen, 8
1028 Howard Street Apartments, Mercy Services

Blessing

May it snow in San Francisco.
May the fishes talk to you.
May the sharks not eat people.
May the homeless have houses.
May you sleep in the clouds.
May your heart beat like a song.
May people not sweat in the summer.
May you swim in spaghetti.
May you travel in space.
May people not drown.
May your clothes glow in the dark.
When you get cut, may you not bleed.
May yams turn to hams.
May you be able to pick up a table with one finger.
May there be no guns.
May your world be full of shiny crystal pearls.
May your heart come out and see heaven.

Janay Brown, 8
Jacqueline Beck, 10
Joseph Beck, 11
Calvin Nguyen, 11
Lily Nguyen, 10
Phillip Nguyen, 8
Mina Vuong, 10
1028 Howard Street Apartments, Mercy Services

Never
Safe

FROSTBITE
What ARE you, a BOY or a GIRL?!
I said, what ARE you?!
High-Waters!! ha ha ha!
hey everyone- Nina doesn't wear a bra!! NO BRA!!
eeew!!
"training bra"

THEY UNLOCKED THE DOORS OF URBANA JUNIOR HIGH AT 7:55 AM. YOU HAD TO BE IN CLASS BY 8:00, GIVING YOU A 5-MINUTE WINDOW. IF YOU GOT TO SCHOOL EARLY (AND YOU HAD TO), YOU WAITED IN A TINY FOYER WITH 1,400 OTHER KIDS PACKED TIGHTER THAN PASSENGERS ON A MUNI BUS...

...OR, YOU WAITED OUTSIDE IN THE SNOW.

THAT'S HOW I GOT FROSTBITE.

A TRUE STORY BY Nina Paley © 4-2000

Every Day

The worst thing
about school is
we have to be
quiet
we have to
follow rules
we have to
get up in the morning
we have the same classes
every day
we have to see
the same people
we have to go
the same route
every day

we have to
do this
and that
whatever
our teachers
say
do this
do that
say this
write that
and I hate
it.

Jessica Clary, 12
Everett Middle School

Being Abandoned

I am a child
with nowhere to go.
I have been abandoned
by my family.
I am sitting
in an alleyway
near a dumpster
watching a drunk man
come close to me.
I am a child
with worries,
worries that I
will be
all alone.

Monique Chanduvi, 13
Everett Middle School

Empty Space

The worst thing about my life
is wondering about my heritage.

How can I feel happy and free
when I'm always wondering
if my real mom's looking for me?

Nowhere to start,
no culture to follow,
I guess all there is
for me is tomorrow.

Behind my happy, laughing face
is a soul that feels hollow,
like an empty space.

They don't know what to call me,
but why should I care?
When asked what I am,
I just give a blank stare.

It seems like it shouldn't matter,
like it ain't even there,
so I don't understand
why I even care.

Keirra Kwan-Hull, 14
Phoenix Middle School

El Oh Vee Ee

My name is love
My name is love
My name is love
My name is love
Love is pain
Love is clear
Love is flexible
Love is pitiful
Love is crazy
My name is love
My name is love
My name is love
My name is love
Love is family
Love is friends
Love is Ginuwine
Can't you see?
Can't you see?
Can't you see?

Love is candy in the rain
Love is a four-page letter
Love is anything
Love is anywhere
Can't you see?
Can't you see?
Can't you see?
Love is ghetto
How so?
I don't know
You don't know
You don't know
You don't know

Paulesha Pulliam, 14
Cache Colvin, 14
Monique Ontiveros, 18
Girls After School Academy

Don't Just Watch Television

I always tell my brother,
don't just watch television.
Write a letter.
Do something.
Imagine that you're flying real high
like a plane
to get out of this place.
Imagine you're flying to another country
or another world.
Don't just sit here watching television.

Anthony Urbina, 12
Everett Middle School

Me, the Magician

I am a magician.
I turn frogs to tigers in an instant.
I make my dinner disappear when I don't like it.
I turn my brother into an ant when he's annoying.
I make real money with the snap of my fingers.
I make candy with the clap of my hands.

Aileen Chea, 12
Everett Middle School

Healer of Natoma

I. THE HEALED

Healer of Natoma
can feel the person's pain.
In his mind, he sees
images of the
person, he can feel
the pain in his heart.

Walking in the woods,
he appears to me
as my aid.
He kneels beside me
as he stretches his arm.
Flow of white light
pours into my heart.

II. MR. EPIDEMIC

A life in a sewer and
an enemy that cures.
"I hate it all," I would say.
I laugh that my breath
of air and poison

makes a flower die
from its living life.
I love my germs. Cruelty.
Bias. Despair. I love to
spread them out to the world.

III. THE HEALER'S MOTHER AND FATHER

They love their son,
only he's a teenager.
"He may get A's but he's very
unusual and silent
within," the parents say.
"Maybe he needs a
girlfriend," the mother says.
The parents always talk about
the son during the night.
"Maybe friends," the father says.
"For what he is,
he's still our little
boy. He's kind of unusual,
but we still love him."

IV. HEALER OF NATOMA

I am a healer
with your love
to the world and others,
in your heart they
work both ways.

My love goes to the world and others.

Our hope may break
like a broken vase,
but the soul is
filled with joy.

The temple is our soul.
For that we are
beautiful in other ways.

If you help others,
your soul is kind.

Vicente Nalam, 14
ArtSpan/Inner City Public Art Projects for Youth

For Real

Mom,
I love you for real
because you are the *Real Deal*.

You are like a diamond in the sea.
You brighten up my days, years, months, and weeks.

You fill my life with
Joy, Happiness and (last but not least) Love.

Even in pain,
you are with me.
For sure.

Mom,
I love you for real
because you are the *Real Deal*.

Sidney Faataui, 13
Phoenix Middle School

Never Safe

Murder,
seeing people in body bags,
hearing about the latest gang fight
or rape,
finding needles or a bullet
on the ground,
knowing you're never safe,
feeling you have nowhere
to belong,
being an outsider,
never staying one place
really long.
Hearing about the world
and its problems.
Running the race
never to win.
Knowing that people aren't even
your friends.

Every so often you hear someone yell,
or maybe you see someone being
violated,
manipulated,
underestimated,
and still you don't stop
and help.
The first thing we think is
he deserved it or maybe
he is just playing.
But it's not all that funny
when it's you or me.

Jermaine LeBrane, 13
Everett Middle School

Sadness

Sadness
always has tears
running down
her beautiful brown skin.
She stares at the stars
and wonders
about the horrible things
that have happened to her.
Oh, what pain she feels.
Her friends
are soft pillows
ready for her
to fall back
on them.

Jennifer Diaz-Romero, 14
Columbia Park Apartments, Mercy Services

Where My Beauty Comes From

I have my mother's eyes
and my father's sensitivity.
I have my gramma's smile
and my grandmother's high, proud cheekbones.
I have my granpa's words
and my grandfather's light brown skin.
I have my aunt's smart mouth
and my cousin's dark magenta lips.
I have my uncle's humor
and my cousin-brother's style.
I have my own intelligence, which
I shall pass down to my own child.

Sadaf Minapara, 14
Columbia Park Apartments, Mercy Services

Kalu

Black is Anthony, the person who is talking now.
Black is beautiful, like everyone here.
Black is a color that no one understands.
Black is cold like when you shiver in the snow.
Black is someone like you and me.
Black can fly like a bird in the sky.
Black is shiny like the sun upon us.
Black is a flower.
Black is Anthony, the one who finished the poem.

Anthony Miller, 12
Everett Middle School

Gangster

I am a young student living in the ghetto.

I see people fighting in the street
about who are better gangs.
I see people doing drugs on the street corner
trying to hide on the side of a car.
I see people shooting in the street
about their color.

I am a young, scared student.

As I walk toward the 19 Polk bus stop,
I see people staring at me real bad
'cause of my race.
I see people following me
and asking me for a dollar.

I am a young, scared student.

Living in a ghetto
is not that easy.

Philip Bautista, 14
Mission High School

Summer Camp

At night,
I looked at the heavens,
I saw the gloomy black night.
I looked at my dreams.
I saw a good poem.

Joshua Renigen, 12
Everett Middle School

The Animals in My Feelings

There is a rabbit in me.
It is a snow rabbit.
It is my peaceful feeling.

There is a cat in me.
It is for anger and for fighting.
It helps me defend myself.

There is a cheetah in me.
It helps me feel powerful.
It is powerful to work
my whole body.

There is a bat in me
that makes me sleepy.
It also makes me wander
dark places at night.

Tung Nguyen, 13
1028 Howard Street Apartments, Mercy Services

Red and Death

Yesterday I was red.
Death is red. Violence
is gangs. Trouble is gangs.
Drugs are worse than eating
a big bug. Drugs cause death.
If I die I pray that I will
go to heaven. Kill is what
gangs do with guns and knives.
The world is dangerous
because of gangs. Someday
I will be dead because
of gangs. I would rather sleep
and kiss my mother.

Cynthia Lopez, 12
Everett Middle School

The Mystery of Cheetahs

No one knows what a cheetah is.
All we know is that cheetahs are swift,
brilliant, graceful, pretty, and cunning.

Cheetahs move through the jungle
with poise and attitude
until,
one day,
out of nowhere,

BANG!

Cheetah handbag.

Don't laugh.
It isn't funny.

Elizabeth Thompson, 12
Everett Middle School

No Gumbo for Me

The first time I had gumbo
I thought it would be nasty,
but my grandmother said,
"It's good."

I was five years old.
I didn't really know
what she was talking about.

I said,
"I don't want that.
It stinks."

My grandma said,
"My gumbo does not stink."

So I had some from my Grandpa's bowl.
It was so good.

I told my grandma,
"Sorry,"
because I really did like it.

So I asked her,
"Can I have some more?"

She said,
"Yes, you can,
Miss Smart Mouth."

Paulesha Pulliam, 14
Girls After School Academy

Chisme/Gossip

There's this chisme about my grandma and grandpa,
before my mother and all of her brothers and sisters were born.
Somebody told my aunts and uncles
and I've heard them talking about it
when this cousin from L.A. visits.
What I've heard is that my grandpa had a big crush on my grandma,
but my grandma had this boyfriend and she hated my grandpa.
Supposedly, my grandpa had to do something
so that my grandma would fall in love with him.
My family says that my grandpa found this witchcraft book
near some tree and that he was doing all these weird things with it.
I've asked my family, "What did he do? Did he drink something?
Did he make her drink something?"
But they didn't know or wouldn't tell me.
Anyway, I think my grandpa gave her some kind of herb thing.
And just like that, my grandma dumped the other guy
and went running to my grandpa's arms.

Dalia Citlali Garcia Mantanez, 14
YWCA Mission Girls Services

I'm Blue

Blue is happy.
Blue looks like it listens to you.
Blue is shy and holds me.
I guess blue is like
a boy at Everett
named Donald.

Donald Murphy, 13
Everett Middle School

School Fears

The day I started to know about things was when I was five years old. I went to kindergarten at Marshall School. I started to cry when my Mom left me at school and came home. I was thinking, Will she come back and pick me up? Will I have to stay here forever?

When school was over and my Mom came to pick me up, I was very mad at her. I hit her. I screamed, "You lied to me! I thought that you were going to stay here with me!"

Days have passed. Years have passed. For another first day of school, I was not scared. I liked it. Fifth grade was hard, fun, and exciting. I had very good friends there like Terry, Peach, and Ronnie. They helped me with my math, science, and spelling tests.

Time passed very fast like a blink of an eye. At graduation, people in my class cried but some didn't. I didn't. I was glad because I was going to go to a new school. I wanted to get out of fifth grade.

It was scary to go to middle school because my friend Bobby told me that you might get beat up if you're small or a new kid. I went to Everett. It was so hard compared to elementary. We had to read bigger books and do more complicated math. I didn't get beat up.

Tai Tran, 14
Mission High School

What I See Daydreaming

Looking into the chalkboard,
it looks like someone just erased it.
But to me it looks like a dragon with spikes,
pushing their way out of the dragon's body.
If you move your head,
it looks like a fish pond.
If you blink your eyes fast,
it's an elephant.

Sarah Villeda-Holmes, 12
Everett Middle School

Walkin'

I've been walkin' all my life,
but I don't know where I'm headed.
People ask me why I'm walkin'
but I just say, "Forget it."
People say my walkin' days are over,
but I keep on walkin'
and quit the talkin'.
I want to walk some more,
but my feet are sore.
Is it because I've walked
from door to door?

Wait a minute.
My feet are no longer sore.
Look, this is the right door.
Have I finally reached the place
after my feet were sore,
after I walked city to city,
day after day?

I think it is.
I think this is the right way.

**Johnny Herrera, 12
Everett Middle School**

Please Tell Me Why

Oh, please tell me, I just can't understand,
why are some people ashamed
of who they really are?
Why do we say, "Why did I have to come
from that country?"
Why do Latino people think that we are
nothing just because we come from
different cultures and countries,
like El Salvador, Guatemala, Mexico or Honduras?
Why are we ashamed of who we really are?
Is it because society doesn't treat us as equals?
Is it because we have different color skin?
Oh, please tell me why people that are immigrants
feel bad because they don't have their papers.
Tell me why, please tell me why people think
they're better than us just because they're citizens.
Ask yourself why.

Liliana Ayala, 13
Everett Middle School

Family Hair

In my family
I'm the only one with straight hair.
My Mom's hair is not so curly,
but not as straight as mine.
When I was five or six years old,
I wanted to have hair like my Mom's
because when we walked in the streets
and it began to rain,
my Mom's hair became curly,
especially the hair in front of her face.
When my little brother was born
he had beautiful hair.
I remember when his hair
was a little bit too long so that it was curly.
I loved to touch his hair.

When he took a bath
and his hair was still wet,
I used to play with his hair.
I told my Mom
that I wanted to have his hair.
When my little brother was five years old,
he was going to start kindergarten
so he had to cut his hair.
Then he began to like short hair.
He has short hair now,
but I can still see his curly hair.
Maybe that is why I love my little brother.

Belen Gonzalez, 14
Mission High School

Gray

sad as a plant that's brown and dying
sad when the sky is gray as cement
sad when the trees are dry as a desert
sad when a bird's wing is broken like glass
sad when I'm broke like the homeless

Angelica Ochoa, 13
Everett Middle School

Hope

Gangs use drugs.
Gangs hope on violence
to take their anger out,
help them forget about
abusive parents,
poverty.
I guess they can't dream
of their parents' love.
Maybe if they ask their parents
at home, tears in their eyes.

Jimmy Phetthiraj, 12
Everett Middle School

Hey, Hey, Hey

Listen,
this time listen with your heart!
Now,
take a deep breath
and let it out with a
Hey, Hey, Hey!
Say Hey to those slaves in Africa,
to those who suffer in
India, Ethiopia, and Eritrea.
They want to be free.
Say Hey to those who starve for hunger.
Please,
feed them.
Shall this continue any longer?
STOP committing this deadly sin.
Say Hey to those who live in Vietnam.
These people die because of wars and crime.
They have a voice.
Listen to them
and every word they have to say.
Think hard about
what they have gone through.

If you don't want to listen,
DON'T!
But later on in life you will realize
how much you were missin'.
Go on,
keep killing these people.
But what goes around
always comes around.
You'll reap what you sow.
From all nations and tribes,
peoples and tongues,
these are the ones,
the ones that have faith!
Faith that they will survive.
They give their lives
to preach and teach while
we sit and tell lies!
What accomplishments have we reached?
It's a shame that they suffer death
while we kick back and rest
and we think we have so little time!
Please,
somebody please, tell me why,

why do we have to live this life
where we suffer with strife?
WHY is there so much violence?
This question
races in your mind every time
and right when you think
that question was answered,
your face brings on
a sign of death,
as you walk into the streets
and see MORE violence!
Why don't people come to realize
all of the DREAMS,
FUTURES,
and
LIVES
inside?
And no matter how hard you try,
you can NOT take their dignity away!
Now, say
HEY, HEY, HEY
to those who have the PRIDE!

Qiana Powell, 13
Everett Middle School

The River

The river is long
like time's drift,
going fast like
blowing wind,
going forever like
the growth of friendship,
ending as life stops.

James Brown, 12
Everett Middle School

In My Neighborhood

In my neighborhood
I hear
laughing
kids shouting
nature
televisions
a car alarm
screaming
barking
next-door neighbors
fire trucks
rustling in the wind
the garbage man
a tea kettle
people lighting a match
drums
street-cleaning trucks
a toilet
a baby crying.

I smell
chow mein
cigarettes
plants
dog food
people smoking on the bus
people playing in the park
bad feet
chicken
sweat in the armpits
stinky people
fresh air
perfume.

I touch
the toilet
a chair
the violin when I practice it
a door when I'm opening it
a desk
a math book
the stove
a pencil.

I see
dogs biting dogs
people walking
our neighborhood
friends
cars
people selling drugs to each other
stores
trees
dogs
skyscraper buildings
Walgreens
Rite Aid
an apple
a wagon
blood
a shirt
firecrackers.

I taste
bacon
pizza
cereal
eggs
oatmeal
Rice Krispies
tuna sandwiches
milk
peanut butter and jelly
apple juice
orange juice
chocolate ice cream
my tongue.

The Poetry Class, Third–Fifth Grades
Career Resources Development Center

Questions of the Universe

I wonder why
the world is
the way
it is.

I wonder why
people live
and they die.

I wonder when
the secrets
of the universe
will be
revealed.

Michael Renigen, 12
Everett Middle School

The Greatest Player

I am a someone
who has a talent.
I like to play basketball
and I am good at it.
I am an all-star
that plays point guard and forward.
I play for Everett Middle School
and when I play I feel proud and excited.
I am someone who is 5 feet 9 inches.
My team has a game today
and I am so excited
I can't sit still.

André Richmond, 14
Everett Middle School

Nani

She is the bright orange,
orange as the evening sun.
She smells like the early morning breeze.
She is the soft sound of clattering dishes
when they are being washed.
She moves slowly through the long narrow balcony,
one step carefully at a time.
She sits by the window reading the Koran
with her cat, Manju, next to her,
brushing her fur through Nani's feet.
She wears a thin white salwar kamiz
with tiny blue flowers and lacey lace,
plain white pants with a nylon ordni
that goes on her head, loops around her neck
with the end hanging down her chest.
Her feet are covered with thin rubber chappals
that clap against her feet each time she walks.

She has a tiny purse with crisp rupees and coins
and the key to the house that she tucks in her bra strap
with a pink handkerchief called a ramal.
In her nose, she wears a big flowerlike nose pin
with red and white rubies.
She dreams about the day
that we will come back from school in Bombay,
where I live with my parents and other grandma.
She dreams about filling
the basketlike jars that hang from the ceiling
with freshly made butter biscuits
bought from the store by the river.
She will say, "Jali gahri aha,"
Come home early.

Asefa Subedar, 14
Columbia Park Apartments, Mercy Services

I Wish

I wish that everyone would live in peace.
I wish that there would be no more school shootings.
I wish that everyone would be smart and go far in life.
I wish that there would be no more kidnapping and murder.
I wish that everyone would live in happiness.
I wish no one would call me names.
I wish that people would respect one another.
I wish that kids would have a voice in this world.
I wish that people would not judge others by their color
         and how they look.
That's what I wish.

Whitney Spencer, 12
Everett Middle School

I Am
Everything
to Me

Two Histories

Daddy wanted to name me Wilhemina after his mother.
You know you're supposed to name your baby after someone who's gone,
not alive.
But then my mother protested.
I should carry her mother's name, Anne.
"Rachel" kept me from the arguments and sour family disputes,
but did it compromise or anger both sides?
And that's what I'm stuck with,
every day
every move
I am a compromise
light skin
but thick bone structure
half 'n' half Jewish girl who fights for BSU* unity
latkes and greens

*BSU stands for Black Student Union.

the horah and the butterfly
act White
won't date Black men
thinks she's better
has good hair
looks more Latina than half-breed
but that boy always called me mixed in such an ugly way
some say, "Nigga get off the swing"
others say, "You're really not like those other Black people"
and I get told it's better to pretend I'm White
but I got two histories in me
both enslaved
and both warriors.

Rachel Bolden-Kramer, 16
Center for Young Women's Development

Keeping It Real

For my daughter

I'm in the Bahamas
peepin' at all the fine guys passing by,
folks swimmin' in the warm water,
sippin' fancy drinks...

No, hold up...

I'm in the movies with my homegirls,
drinking soda and eating popcorn,
big drama lighting up the big screen,
a moment's escape from the drama of my own life...

That ain't right either...

I'm at home taking care of my baby daughter,
hearing her laugh, watching her grow.
Her first steps, her first words...

But even that ain't happening...

I'm only there in my dreams.
The cute guys, the fancy drinks, kicking it at the movies,
being there with my daughter.
I wake up and it's all gone...

In place of all that are the deputies,
the four corners, and loneliness.

The only beach I see is loneliness.
The only companion for a convict is misery.
And the only time I'm holding my baby girl is during official visits.

Thirty minutes at a time
is not enough time.

Sarah A., 15
Phoenix Middle School

On the Underground Bus

Hey, Miss.
Excuse me.
You just bumped into me.
Nah, I'm not going to say nothin'.
You just hurry on to your 40-dollar-an-hour job
and I'll be on my way.
Yeah, hurry on.
Don't wanna be late
as you storm off clutching your espresso in one hand
and Coach bag in the other.
I admire your French manicure.
Go on, girl, strut your stuff.
Someday that may be me bumping into people
walking fast to my 40-dollar-an-hour job
clutching my Coach bag in one hand
and espresso in the other,
with my French manicure,
and my fitted clothes.

Hey, Miss.
Excuse me.
You just bumped into me
Without a head turn
or a sorry.
I may be nothing to you
but I am everything to me.

Stephanie Sabini, 16
Center for Young Women's Development

Nobody Knows

I think nobody knows I like sports
because I am fat.
People think I hate to move.
I used to ski back in Japan,
felt like I was flying.
You look at me and see fat boy.
You think lazy.

Shuai Liu, 16
Newcomer High School

The Wind Blows Me

I remember
my hometown is small as a bird.
Birds fly in the sky
as I play on the ground.

I remember the farm,
my family's treasure.
I used to plant cabbages, corn, and rice.

I remember the streets are not wide,
but they are clean.

I remember the air is freshness.

I can hear the birds singing songs.

I can visit another town with my friends.

I remember the wind blows me
to San Francisco.

Ju Xian Li, 16
Newcomer High School

Have You Ever?

Have you ever had to steal so you can eat dinner?
Have you ever had a teacher say,
　　　"You'll never be a winner"?

Have you ever watched your best friend
　　　shoot himself in the head?
Have you ever gotten a call saying
　　　someone you love is dead?

Have you ever wished that you could die?
Have you ever been so sad you couldn't cry?

Have you ever had a big problem
that just kept getting bigger?
Have you ever had your heart stop
　　　because you drank too much liquor?

Have you ever been in reality, but still in a dream?
Have you ever done something good,
but still felt like leaving the scene?

Have you ever seen your Mom cry so much
　　　that you wanted to kill?
Have you ever been healthy
　　　but still felt ill?

Marcus O., 17
Log Cabin Ranch

No Paper No Books

for The Rev. Martin Luther King Jr.

When I heard Black children's classrooms
had no chairs
no paper
no books
and no pens
I felt angry like you.
I am a person of color in America too.
I see things are not equal.

Before I came here,
I believed all people would be equal
in America
because your dream came true.
But we need to work hard
to keep the dream alive.

Jia Jian Lin, 17
Newcomer High School

A.B.C.

我
是
美
国
长
大
的
中
国
人

I was born in the United States of America.

Therefore, I'm an American,
an American Born Chinese.

But why do people still stereotype me
for who I am?

They tell me to go back to China.
They say I'm a dog eater.
They say that I swam to the U.S.

They say that I'm an illegal immigrant.

But why?
I was born in America.
I live life the American way.
I went to an American public school.
I speak, write, and read English,
just like any other American.

The only thing different about me
is my skin color,
the shape of my eyes,
and my lifestyle.

I am an American,
an American Born Chinese.

我
是
美
国
长
大
的
中
国
人

Raymond T., 17
Log Cabin Ranch

A Girl Wonders

What if
there is no school
but there is still something to learn?

What if
there is no school
but there is a teacher
ready to teach?

What if
there is no school
but a student wants to know
what's going on with her
community and world?

What if
there are lots of questions
that I like to ask
but there is no one
who can answer them?

Jinile Calpe, 16
Mission High School

Love Jones

I know this girl who's so fine,
her look and smell will blow your mind.
The sound of her voice will thrill your bones.
Oh yes! Ladies and Gentlemen,
I have a LOVE JONES.

About 5 foot 6, 165 pounds,
she's not thin, because I like them round.
She's black, BOLD, and beautiful,
everything to me,
that's why our love will last an eternity.
A joyous celebration for the new year
we will work out our anger and all our fears.
Because we have to dodge them haters like orange cones
and continue our LOVE JONES.

My love for her is more serious than hay fever
because she knows that I will never leave her.
Even though the haters have it in their bones,
they can't stop my LOVE JONES.

**Marcus O., 17
Log Cabin Ranch**

The Women Before Me

I owe the power behind my voice to my ancestors.
Although they've passed,
my voice carries their power and dignity.
I owe my strength to myself.
Growing up to be 15,
I've had to experience
what many may say is nothing,
but I am a woman, a girl, a modest person, and a fighter.
I think that deep down inside I owe myself thanks,
thanks for trying to show the real me
and expressing my opinions and thoughts.
I owe the symbols of my survival to my sister, Ana.
She defends me and stands up for herself
in restaurants and stores.
I owe the woman I have become to my Mom.
Unlike me, she stands out in the presence of a crowd.
My Mom gave me my mad temper
which, in a way, is good.
She showed me everything there is to know
about being natural, being my own person.

Veronica de los Angeles Orozco, 15
YWCA Mission Girls Services

Leaving China

To say goodbye
words sick at my heart
my tears would not drop out.

Jia Hua Miao, 16
Newcomer High School

Work for Change

for The Rev. Martin Luther King Jr.

You worked for people of color,
died for your great work.
We will remember you forever.
Now people of color have more power than before.
"Whites Only" sign,
no longer on the restaurant's door.
We can sit in any seat on the bus.
Even the mayor of San Francisco is not a White man.

Of course there is not total equality.
The White people and the rich
may look down on the colored and poor.
The United States has changed but still is unfair.
People from other countries do not
have as much power as people born here.
We have a lot of work to do to make all people equal.

Penelope Zheng, 17
Newcomer High School

Locked-Up Thoughts

When I'm locked up, I have plenty of time
because all I'm doing is time.

While doing that time, my head is filled
with nothing but thoughts.

There is nothing better to do than think.

I think about what I did.

I think about why I did what I did.

I do nothing but wonder how I got caught.

Every day I also think about the things I'll do
when I get out,
or the things I could do
if I was out.

But do you know what the worst thought to me is,
the thought that's constantly running through my mind?

It's when I see someone leave
and say to myself,
"When is it my turn?"

Raymond T., 17
Log Cabin Ranch

Chinatown

The night is quiet,
nobody in the street.
In the morning
I see people working,
I hear people shouting.
In the market
I smell vegetables, pork, and every kind of fish.
I see many people buying food for lunch and dinner.

In Chinatown
I see many Chinese people,
I hear Chinese words.
In Chinatown
I feel intimacy.
It lets me float back to China.

Helen Liang, 17
Newcomer High School

Retrofit Man

There was a big storm.
I got electrified from the lightning
when I was reaching
my hand up in the air.
Later, powers that looked
like lightning came out of them.
I tested them out.
Boy, did I do cool tricks with them.
I could lift up a big tall building.
I could tie things up
so they didn't fall.
I really tested my powers
when I saw the biggest earthquake.
My powers stopped things
from falling down.
Finally I'm a superhero.
That's how I became Retrofit Man.

Matthew Stark, 16
ArtSpan/Inner City Public Art Projects for Youth

Night and Day

In China
the night is warm
the sky has many stars
and a big moon.
In the city I hear families laugh
the insects singing
and the music
slow moving.

Morning in the market
I smell the flowers fragrant
the candies sweet
the mango the watermelon.
I see many colors of ice cream
many packs of chips
and people crowding in
to buy them.

Liu-Fen Zeng, 16
Newcomer High School

Abuelita Birra

Who's Abuelita Birra?

Is she that Pink Rose who gave birth to my mother?

Is Abuelita Birra that Pink Rose
who has mariposas, claveles, árboles de naranjas in her garden?

Who every day at five in the morning wakes up
and gets her hose and regando las plantas?

Who's Abuelita Birra?

That Rosada Rosa, every time a grandchild is born, a new rose blooms
      in her garden.

People in the morning see her in her flowered dress and guaraches
clipping the dead roses, feeding the living ones.

When the sun comes out, it always comes to that beautiful
      Pink Rose's house.

Lizzeth Carmona, 15
Columbia Park Apartments, Mercy Services

For My Father

Every morning when I wake up I cry.
I ask myself, *Why did you have to die?*

I try to put it all in the past,
but the memory of you, your absence
and my own agony

make me want to die.

You used to say,
"No matter how hard life gets,
don't give up!"

You used to wake me up with a morning kiss,
calling me "Angel" or "Shorty."

You would laugh and joke a lot,
and I was so happy.

We used to go for long walks
and talk about life
as we watched the sunset.

You had a wonderful life.
Were you out of your mind?

Drinking and driving,
that's a terrible way to die.

I cry and cry
and ask myself, *Why?*

Katya Romero, 16
Ida B. Wells High School

The Seasons Back Home

I remember Spring,
our garden flowers opening,
butterflies and bees circling.

I remember Summer,
our pond giving up its water to the Sun,
a sweet rain filling it up again.

I remember Fall,
our garden flowers gone,
the tree leaves changing clothes,
green becoming yellow and orange.

I remember Winter,
our pond giving its water to the thirsty earth,
just some small fish in the pond.

I am smiling
full of memories.

Zhen Wen Zhang, 17
Newcomer High School

FOUR

Seeing
Clearly

HURDLES

by Derek Kirk

I jump hurdles every day. While everyone else on the track team runs straight through, my fellow hurdlers and I go up and down, up and down. Some hurdlers jump over the hurdles, and others kick them down. I jump over them.

Sometimes I'd like to just kick them out of my way, but I guess I'm just too polite. But who cares, I can cross the finish line and that's all that matters. Besides, my coach says either way is just fine.

We call our coach "Pear-Nose". There's always a pair of black sunglasses atop that nose of his. And he always stands with his hands behind his back. Now that I think about it, I've never seen his hands. Maybe he doesn't have any hands, I don't know.

He drove us especially hard this one particular practice before a track meet with a rival high school. We circled the track, around and around, endlessly. Anyone who stepped off that beaten track was punished with more laps.

Finally, I couldn't go on anymore without water, so I parted from my lane and ran to the drinking fountain.

When I turned around, Pear-Nose was staring down at me.

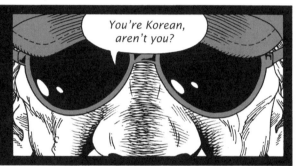

You're Korean, aren't you?

Yes.

How did you know?

Because the Chinese are smart.

I was struck speechless. Then he told me to run back onto the track. I started to run. I ran through the grass, past the baseball field, out of the main gate, and straight to my house.

I jump hurdles every day.

Leave Me Alone

I'm the purple-haired punk rocker girl
who always tried to be different.
The one who people capped on
for being weird.

Why do you dye your hair?
Why do you pierce yourself?
Why don't your clothes match?
Why are you acting white?

Well, here are answers for your stupid questions:

Because I can.
Because I want to.
Because I don't care what you think.
Because it's none of your business.

Here is a question for you:
Are you me?
No!
Then don't worry
about what I do.

Sarah Castro, 18
YWCA Mission Girls Services

What You See

The girl they see is crazy,
but the woman I am just overreacts at times.

The girl they see is a tomboy,
but the woman I am likes to have fun.

The girl they see is nosy,
but the woman I am is curious about people and who they are.

The girl they see is strong,
but the woman I am wants to be more than that.

The girl they see is a smartass,
but the woman I am takes things personally and gets defensive.

The girl they see is sweet,
but the woman I am sometimes needs to be serious.

The girl they see is sexy,
but I am just a woman.

Bernadette Lopez, 20
YWCA Mission Girls Services

Ode to My Period

The first time I got my period
was the day I became a woman.

I must have been 13,
or something like that.

Damn, was I really that young?

But I remember it
like it was yesterday.

I know that during the day
I was fenning for some candy,
just anything.

I remember that my Mom
came home around seven that night.

So I go to the toilet
to do my pee-pee thing
and I wipe
and, when I look,
I see blood.

I thought,
Oh my God
se me rompió
mi cosita.

So I run
to my Mom's bedroom
with my chionies
down to my ankles.

I say,
*Mama
me rompi,
estoy sangrando.
I'm gonna die.*

At that moment
my Mama
must have given
me a look like,
Guess what you got?

Next thing I knew
everyone in my family knew,
including my Dad.

My Mom called my tías, my tíos
and even my abuelos in El Salvador.

It was like a big ol' celebration:
La niña agarró la menstruación.

My Mom and I even went out to
eat Chinese food that night.

It was really weird.
My Mom started explaining
how to use a pad
and even tried to school me
about tampons.

Hell's naw, I thought.
I ain't putting nothing
up my cosita.
No toxic shock syndrome for me!

But that was the day
that I became a woman.

Maybe not a woman mentally,
but spiritually, yes,
I was a woman.

Lydia Celis, 19
YWCA Mission Girls Services

The Ghetto Curse

U say u want to be a thug
on the corner, slangin' drugs.
Was it a lack of luv?
Now u want to fill a brother with slugs.
Just because u packin' a gat
doesn't mean u got it like that.
Live by the gun u die by the gun,
that is a fact.
Gettin' yo head pumped up off a rap,
then u go out there and get smoked like a joint.
Now let me get to the point.
If you continue the ghetto curse
u might just end up in a hearse.

Dartanian K., 18
Log Cabin Ranch

Counting the Ways

My family is a blessing when we are yelling
at the top of our lungs,
fighting and arguing
and being the loudest Mexicans on the block.

My family is a blessing when we all get together
on Easter and crack flour eggs on each other's heads.

My family is a blessing when we all get together
and go delirious, act stupid and laugh till our stomachs hurt
and we're crying, in tears.

My family is a blessing when we get together
for special events,
like to plan my sista's baby shower.

My family is a blessing when after seeing a scary movie
like *The Blair Witch Project*
Tina wants to sleep in my room.

My family is a blessing when someone wants
to borrow money from you.

My family is a blessing when my cousin
wanna whip on her baby's daddy.

My family is a blessing when we have
our Mother/Daughter Days or Sister Days.

My family is a blessing when we say goodbye
to each other, we always cry.

My family is a blessing 'cause,
damn, I have a big family!

My family is a blessing when me and my sister
get on my Dad's nerves.

My family is a blessing 'cause there's no other family
like my family.

Andrea Rodriguez, 21
YWCA Mission Girls Services

Panyu

Panyu rains in the Spring.
People stay home,
farmers begin to cultivate.
I feel bored when it rains.

In the Summer
people like to swim
because it is so hot.
Farmers are harvesting
and cultivating again.
I like swimming.
I feel tired on the hot days.

In the Fall
people are crowded in the downtown.
They walk watching
working
shopping.
Farmers harvest again.
I feel cool and comfortable.
I love the Fall.

In the Winter
all the leaves
fall down from trees.
The weather becomes cold.
People stay home
in Panyu
where I'm from.

Simon Chen, 18
Newcomer High School

Invasion

You all need to stop invading
and stop parading.
This is our hood, our homes.
Can't you get that through your domes?
We only have one district
and this is it.
Can't you see that you don't fit?
What? You enjoy watching us go
cuz rent is too rich and we too poor.
Ya'll got money, go elsewhere.
This is what we can afford.
Ain't that fair?

Tell me something.
Does it put a smile on your face
to see the Mission invaded with fancy cafés?
Does it make you happy to see more of your kind?
Please, do tell me what goes on in those wicked li'l minds.
Let me guess, it's reach.
Nah, uh, it's got to be a goal
to see the beautiful people of the Mission go.

You know it kills me
to see my people struggle and strive,
to keep a roof over they heads

and food on the table to keep alive,
messed up homes with no heater.
What? Air conditioning?
Nah, we ain't got none of that either,
but we don't complain
cuz we can't afford more.
So let us keep our mouths shut
about broken windows or even a broken door.

You see the point that I am tryna make
is that you all took our homes before.
I guess ya'll got a habit
of taking what's not yours.
But I'm a tell you,
this is more than just a place to sleep.
It's something that goes way too deep,
something that you wouldn't understand,
being that you never could leave colored land.
So once again we are defeated.
But live with the guilt
that you used your color,
so you cheated.

Nez Carrasco, 18
YWCA Mission Girls Services

I Am

I am the daughter of the sweetest juices
and the finest wines of the freshly picked
grapes, peaches, nectarines, and OH YEAH cherries
harvested by hardworking hands and bloodshed tears.

I am the daughter of broken dreams
just trying to survive another nightmare
on these Frisko streets!

I am the daughter of YESTERDAY'S misconception
TODAY'S misled directions and
TOMORROW'S dirty elections
but
I will RISE in RESURRECTION!

I am the daughter of the Howling MOON
and Yearning SUN
who will embrace the world
and enlighten my life.

I am the daughter of BREATH
contemplating my thoughts as I
envision sounds of MUSIC
running through my body
vibrating the electromatic static
of the TIMBALES playing
SAXOPHONE crying out words
the PIANO twinkling rose petal thoughts
and the CONGAS awakening my spirits
with levels of who I am.

I come from a long line of spiritual warriors
destined to seek the ROOTS of the TRUTH.

I am
IZTICPALOPOC
THE OBSIDIAN
BUDAFLY!!!

Andrea "Budafly" Rodriguez, 21
YWCA Mission Girls Services

To My Daughter, Eliana Alexis

What would I do if I lost you, Mija? Because of you I got my life together. And not because I had to, I wanted to. I wanted to give you everything since the day I found out I was pregnant on August 7, 1997. Your father and I didn't have much to offer, but we found a way, working extra jobs and cutting down on alcohol. I never buy clothes for myself anymore, so you can have toys. Now you even have things you don't want, like your Big Girl Bed. You don't even sleep in it. But what matters is, you didn't ask for things to have us say no, no, no, we can't afford it.

I take your picture because I want to capture your childhood. You're growing up so fast. You're about to turn two! I remember holding you for the first time, 7 pounds 11 ounces. Now, forget it! You're 30 pounds and you hardly ever let me hold you unless you are tired or sick. I don't want you to grow up. I want you to be my baby forever.

You're my pretty girl and you'll forever be my pretty girl. Nothing will ever make that change! If I have more kids, I don't want you to think I love you less. Your baby brother or sister may have more than you did because your dad and I will have better jobs. It's not about love, it's about opportunity. It's because of you I got a job and got off welfare. Because of you, I am still standing instead of ending up in la pinta or dead.

You are my angel, my gift from God, my miracle baby. Please remember that. You are my firstborn and the reason I am alive. I am living for you. My soul belongs to you and your dad. Please remember, I love you, Mija.

Your Mommy

Erica Thorson, 22
Center for Young Women's Development

Ghetto State of Mind

The life I lived is violent
killers, hustlers, playas, and innocent bystanders all in one.
But this is how I chose to live.
Sitting on my block getting money,
being a negative role model for little kids.
Why did I choose to live the way I lived?
Is it because I wanted to thug all my life,
and supply rocks for dope fiends' pipes?
Or is it because I'm trapped in a cage full of rage,
ready to flip the page and go into that savage phase?
I can't call it.

Young cats killing each other over drugs and turfs,
trying to see a mill ticket.
I know my family doesn't want to pick out my casket,
living this life they'll be forced to pick it.
Sometimes when I'm asleep at night I have dreams
of my life coming to an end.
You might call these nightmares, to me these are dreams.
Maybe because it comes with the package,
this life is all hood, caskets are all wood,
this life is too much for me.
Too much killing, too much crime.

Too many young brothas killing their own people
for the price of a dime.
Too many sisters not knowing who they baby daddy is,
because they didn't trip off who they was with
before they handled they biz.
Too many little kids growing up without their fathers;
because they so-called father ran out
because he couldn't handle his responsibility.

But technically that's the way the game goes
when you living this ghetto life,
with struggling and strife,
where you got to fight to win your rights.
'Cause in this life ain't nothing free.
The poor stay poor,
the rich get more chips,
and dope dealers live ghetto fabulous
with all the baddest chicks.

But now, me personally, I'm through with this life of crime.
But can't nobody change my ghetto state of mind.

Charles K., 19
Log Cabin Ranch

You Stood Me Up!

I remember waiting
waiting and waiting
for you to come by
to take me out
but you never showed up!

You called me the day before
and told me
that you were going
to take me out
and spend the day with me.

So the next day
I woke up
and stood there
at the window
till you showed up.

My Mom did my hair
and dressed me up
to see you.

I think my Mom knew
you weren't really
going to show up.

But I waited
and she didn't
tell me anything.

But I waited
and you never showed up,
never even called
to tell me why.

I remember going
to my Mom,
crying,
and asking her
why you didn't show up.

I asked myself,
What had I done?
Were you mad at me?
But the next day
you called.

You lied to me.
You told me that
you were at Nana's house
the whole day
because she was sick.

You stood up your own daughter,
the one who shares
your blood.

My Mom cried for nights,
not because she loved you,
but because she loves me.

It hurt her more
to see me in pain
than herself.

She knew your ways.
You played her too!

But her love and concern
were for me,
not for you.

You stood me up!

Lydia Celis, 19
YWCA Mission Girls Services

The Great Escape

I don't remember much of my kid days, but I was told that when I was about three years old, I used to break out of my crib. My mother and grandma didn't ever know how I did that. So one day, my Mom put me in my bed and watched me to see what I was going to do. She said I laid down for a while, then I looked up and turned around my pillow and put it on the floor. Then I did a front flip over the bars and fell on my pillow. She saw me get up to run into the kitchen, but she said, "Got ya." Then I just sat back down and scratched my head and laid down like I was asleep.

Troy Alexander, 18
Mission High School

Seeing Clearly

I am the stars,
the moon, and the queen of the earth.
I am the ground many folks walk on and litter.
I am the concrete,
spreading miles and miles,
connecting concrete walls.

I am the knife,
the gun,
and the drugs that killed you.
I am the metal structure of your overcrowded building.

I am the 7 cent an hour paid overseas,
the 10 cent an hour paid in my own city.
I am these mean streets, every day.

I am the torture of my slave ancestors,
the ship that kidnapped them.
I am the weave and the braids,
the nappy thick hair,
takes hours to comb.

I am the thought
you think now.
I am the conversation you will have later on tonight.
I am the dream
you do remember.
I am the dream
Martin Luther King Jr. had.

I am the life,
soul, and spirit of a woman.
I am a woman who loves my women.
I am the ignorance you once had.
I am the ignorance I had too.
I am the child with no food to eat,
the child on drugs.

I am those signs held up in a demonstration.
I am the microphone,
loud strong voice.
I am the organizing,
the Power,
the Word.
I am the flyers posted all over town.
I am this revolution.
I am that political prisoner.
I am
I am
I am not blind,
not no more,
I am not blind.

Rasheedah Mahir, 18
Center for Young Women's Development

I Know What They Really Mean

You talented
is what people
that see my outta side say about me.

Don't waste your life
is what people say
that don't like seeing me selling drugs.

You're a hoodlum and a thug
is what I came to believe.
I will be nothing else but what I hear.

I love you
from people that believe in me.
When people mad from me dogging them, they scream
I hate you and
You will never be shit.
I leave them like saliva
from the mouth when you spit.

You are smart, use it.
I like when people tell me this.
It is a compliment,
like when females have me smiling saying,
You hella fine.
When girls tell me this
I know they dudes want to say,
You a punk.
My friends say this to me too, and say

I will always be there for you.

Scott Y., 19
Log Cabin Ranch

Something to Live For

Silence sweeps the room.
I can feel the fire,
the fiery rage
that makes me think shady.
I know I should go calm myself down.
I know my peace has to come
from looking in the eyes of my newborn baby.
So I sit with her by the window
and watch the stray dogs play on the hillside.

If I didn't have my baby girl
I might go insane.
When I think about her
I think about life,
and there goes the sound of a passing train.

Onnie B., 19
Log Cabin Ranch

This Must Not Get Lost

[TEACHERS' WRITINGS]

WANDERING HOME TO THE MISSION

ALWAYS A CHANGIN' SCENE DOWN HERE.

NEW FACES, NEW PERSPECTIVES NEW CLASHES.

IT USED TO BE DIFFERENT WHEN I FIRST GOT HERE.

THE REMNANTS OF THE IRISH COMMUNITY STILL GATHERED AT McCARTHY'S ON ST. PATRICK'S DAY.

McCARTHY'S IS GONE NOW.

It Ain't Taffy

Like those eternal wounds on His hands, head, heart, and feet,
my goal of passing on the Promethean fire is never complete.

After kicking all the incomprehensibles to the curb
and breaking down the cryptics,
it is my hope that these students burn with a hunger
       greater than hunger,
with the painful joy of a life fulfilled.
But there's this one issue blocking the bandwidth
       of this transmission.

How's this stuff gonna get me paid?
Baby's gotta eat. I ain't got time for your metaphors and similes,
or whatever.
Why should I care? Poetry don't pay my bills.

The questions of a young community struggling to survive
are as real as survival itself.

What can you say to a young person whose economic needs
       exceed the time
to reflect?
I want to tell them that poetry will pay the rent
       and all the bills for eternity
and a day,

that it can ease the pain better than any narcotic,
that it can bust you out of this tangled mess of a life
      that wasn't designed for
our kind.
that it will destroy the demons that dominate your dreams,
that it will get you 40 acres, a mule, a mansion, a mercedes,
      and a promise of
never again.
I want to tell them that poetry will make it all make sense.

But what's all that mean to a gangsta shorty trying to stay low,
just trying to stay out of an enemy's cross hairs?
What is poetry to a kid who's tired, hungry, confused, and abused?
To a student who's struggling to sort out the contradiction
      of addiction?
To a student who just lost a parent?
an older brother?
a younger sister?
To a barely literate teenage mother
      who just wants to write love poetry
to her boo locked away in a penitentiary?
To a youngster facing an uncertain future
in a country that has already counted him as a casualty?

Survival is a day-to-day thing. They don't need another dope dealer
to fill their pipes full of hazy, lazy distracting promises,
they don't need another syringe needle filled
                with sweet delectable lies.

I am tempted to stretch the truth,
but the truth ain't taffy.

Can't lie to my students.
Won't set them up for more disappointment.
Got to keep this real.

And this demands that I must *be real*.
So, from within my rib cage,
I offer a humble answer to my students' concerns:

Poetry may not be able to pay the bills
or your taxes or post your bail,
but it shines brighter than that.
Under all the ache of the day-to-day,
beyond the concealed sorrow of this Disneyland life,
within the pumping chambers of your own blood-filled heart,
there is poetry.

a Reality more Real than real estate, an illuminating, liberating Truth
that cannot be incarcerated, impoverished, enslaved or even killed.

Poetry whets your appetite for insight, education, and liberation.
And without this sublime hunger,
your present pain and hunger
may never come to mean anything to anyone.

And when this is discovered,
when you can perceive and receive poetry
as a tangible means to the magic of insight and transformation,
no one will ever be able to take it away from you and yours

… much less charge you rent for it….

Russell (Gonzaga)
Ida B. Wells High School
Phoenix Middle School
Columbia Park Boys and Girls Club, Excelsior Unit

Don't Know What to Say

what do I tell her
my student
comes to class
bloodied and bruised
by her boyfriend
by her girlfriend
do we talk about it
as a class topic
or do I attract and distract
with some other fact of
life
like political prisoners
or how to sample your favorite song in your poem
or anything
anything
but let's not talk about how bad you look
bloodied and bruised
and how I wish I could have been there
take the weapon out of his and her hands
I won't show you
I'm screaming inside and
how much I wanna cry
and you don't either.

what do I tell her
my student
comes to class
bloodied and bruised
by her boyfriend
by her girlfriend
how do I convince her
the pencil
writing words
can free her
not from life's whipping winds
and the burn they make on her skin
but free her mind
from stopping to think
she deserve it.

Ananda Esteva
Center for Young Women's Development
Newcomer High School

Poet Girl

I visited her class once a week last year.
She followed the instructions for every exercise
with excitement and enthusiasm,
maybe even a little joy.
(Isn't that what we teachers want?)
She read her work aloud to her classmates,
without the reward of a silly sticker I offer
those students who grimace and writhe.
I am like a doctor after a measles shot:
"There now, there now."

During lunch, she came to write poetry.
She sat waiting patiently, expectantly.
Other students came to eat,
listen to music.
We teachers fiddled with days and times:
Tuesdays after school.
No, Thursdays at lunch.
Okay, Tuesdays and Thursdays at lunch.

This year, she does not come,
during lunch or after school,
and I am not assigned to one of her classes.

This year, I rarely see her
and only in the halls.
Her clear brown eyes,
hidden with blue plastic.
Her punk rock
interpretation of herself
wraps her in black.

I wonder:
Is she writing her poems?

I remember finding my own salvation
in similar quick beats,
ripped jeans and T-shirts
as I walked these same halls
twenty years ago.
It was that and poetry
that saved me.

What do you say to a student
who shares her heart on paper
then glides away
when you forget to schedule,
to open your mind,
to stop being a teacher and just listen?

I organized a reading
in the library a few weeks ago
and she came.
She wanted to read so badly,
she volunteered to speak someone else's words.
It was a poem.

I hope she'll read this poem too.

I'm glad you haven't given up.
Continue to connect
the light in your soul
with a pen
and carve it into paper.

Cathy Arellano
Mission High School
YWCA Mission Girls Services
Girls After School Academy

I Stole Bryan's Poem

I teach incarcerated students
and I committed this crime:
I wanted his poem
so I took it,
circled the large worktable
and whisked it
right out from under him.

He would never turn in his work
because I typed one of his poems
and hung it on the library wall.
He tore it down,
then came to class more often.

Bryan got dead time that night
trying to get his poem back.
He wouldn't go into the dorm
for the count.

I drove home along the coast
wondering exactly what I was teaching,
he would pay for my crime.
Could I prove to him the worth of his words?

His poem was about being called a nigger.
He broke the word into an acrostic
beginning with N for the "negative impact"
and in pieces, letter by letter,
he countered ignorance with consciousness,
looked at a legacy of loss,
discovered gratitude
for all the people who fought for him,
and felt encouraged.
He realized his actions
are finally most important,
that they can transcend, and resist,
and create his "own fate."
He dismantled the word
and walked into life.

This knowledge must not get lost,
and to preserve it, I stole it.

Now I appeal to justice
to examine our relative crimes.

Bryan continues to pay.

I drive away.

And what of all those
who have used this word
throughout this free country's history.

Justice?
Bryan continues to pay.

Kimberley Nelson
Log Cabin Ranch

Paper Boat

I

He leans his elbows
on his desk,
folds his paper
into squares of decreasing size,
says he isn't writing poetry
today so don't even try
to make him.

II

This is not a story
about salvation.

III

He is in fifth grade.
He slides down banisters
he isn't supposed to,
tells me in the hall
before class
he doesn't have anything
to write about, ever.
He tells me his little sister
ate lead paint
off kitchen walls.
Look, I say,

taking his paper, turning it
this way and that,
it's a boat
or *a red-winged bird.*

IV
There are days I cannot shake
the sense of having failed,
days I want words to lay open
our lives, lure sun
from a defeated sky.

V
He takes the paper boat,
the bird,
shreds it.

Octopus legs, he says,
grinning.

Michelle Matz
Everett Middle School
Career Resources Development Center

Poetry Turned 14 Last Week

Her life will never be as neat
as the stacks of laundry
she folds for her mother.
If Poetry's father would let her,
she'd pierce her nose.
She likes hot chips
from the corner store
and the color orange.
Poetry learned the exact
circumference of the moon
in science class last week.
But late nights,
when she watches it
from her bedroom window,
she knows she could hold it
in her palm like a dime.
Yesterday, Poetry saw a gun
lying in a garbage can
behind her school.
She comes home,
leaves her jeans
in a pile on her bed,

puts on a sea green salwar kamiz
that gathers around
her ankles like the tide.
Poetry's dark eyes shine.
Tell her she's beautiful,
she'll say you're crazy.
Her little sister turns
somersaults under the table
while she writes about the roses
in her abuela's garden.
Poetry might live in an apartment
on Folsom Street,
but notebooks as big as houses
can't contain her words.
Poetry is trilingual.
She speaks one language
with her parents,
another with her friends.
Then there's the language
she dreams in.

Alison Seevak
Mercy Services
ArtSpan/Inner City Public Art Projects for Youth

ABOUT THE ARTISTS

Gabrielle Gamboa discovered comic books in high school after reading the Hernandez Brothers' *Love and Rockets*. She attended art school at the California College of Arts and Crafts, and has since enjoyed creating comic books and illustrations for several Bay Area papers and magazines. Gabrielle was born in Sacramento, California. Her Web site address is www.ladygg.com.

Anson Jew, 36, was born in Sacramento, California. His self-published comic book, *Saturday Nite*, won a Xeric Grant in 1998. After working as an animator at a computer game company for nine years, he is currently a freelance illustrator. His online portfolio site is at www7.bcity.com/ansonart.

Derek Kirk was born in South Korea in 1974. He has lived in the United States since he was 9 years old and is currently living in Korea trying to relearn his first language. Kirk is the writer/artist of a few graphic short stories. They can be read in a xeroxed mini-comic called *Small Stories*. Some of his illustrations can also be found in *Youth Outlook*, shameful vending machine stickers, and in bathroom stalls all across California.

Nina Paley, 32, was born and raised in Urbana, Illinois. In 1988 she moved to Santa Cruz, California, where she debuted "Nina's Adventures" in the *Santa Cruz Comics News* in 1988. It appeared in scores of weekly and alternative newspapers, including the *Funny Times*, the *LA Reader*, and the *San Francisco Weekly*. In1995, Nina developed a mainstream daily strip about cats called "Fluff," which was syndicated internationally by Universal Press Syndicate. In 1998 she quit "Fluff" to return to "Nina's Adventures." Nina is also an illustrator, animator, and designer. Her online portfolio is at www.ninapaley.com.

Spain Rodriguez is currently the primary artist of "The Dark Hotel," Salon.com's online noir comic series about the notorious hotel built in 1893 near San Francisco's Chinatown. He also created the art for *The Manchurian Experiment*, and wrote and created the art for *Murder at the Hey Hey Club*. Spain was born in Buffalo, New York in 1940. You can find "The Dark Hotel" at www.salon.com; click on "comics."